Our World of Water

For my brother Sam,
the sailor

First published in Great Britain in 2008 by Frances Lincoln Children's Books,
4 Torriano Mews, Torriano Avenue, London NW5 2RZ
www.franceslincoln.com

First paperback edition 2008

ISBN: 978-1-84507-973-4

Printed in China
9 8 7 6 5 4 3 2

Oxfam believes that everyone is entitled to a life of dignity and opportunity;
and they work with poor communities, partner organisations in different
countries, volunteers and supporters to make this a reality. Oxfam's Education
and Youth Programme supports this work by enabling children and young
people to understand their world and make a positive difference in it.
www.oxfam.org.uk/education

We would like to thank all the children who took part in *Our World of
Water*, and their families and communities for their enthusiastic support.
We would also like to thank the photographers who spent time with the
six children featured in the book.

Amin from the Drik Photo Agency went to Gaibandha in Bangladesh
to see Saran and his family.

Annie Bungeroth travelled to Ethiopia to take pictures of Gamachu
in his village near the town of Dubluk. Later she flew to Macusani
in Peru to spend time with Lucas.

Caroline Irby visited Tajikistan to take photographs of Barfimoh in the
village of Pista Mazor, near the border with Afghanistan.

Geoff Sayer spent time with Khadija and her family at their home
in Nouakchott, the capital city of Mauritania.

Sungwan So went to see Dahlys in Arcadia, near Los Angeles City,
California, in the USA.

Oxfam GB will receive a royalty for each copy of this
book sold in the UK.

Oxfam is a Registered Charity no. 202918. Oxfam GB
is a member of Oxfam International. Oxfam works with
others to overcome poverty and suffering.

Our World
of Water

Beatrice Hollyer

Foreword by Zadie Smith

F

FRANCES LINCOLN
CHILDREN'S BOOKS

in association with **Oxfam**

Our World

Mauritania: Khadija
I live by the sea, where it is very windy. We keep water in a big pottery jar. My favourite drink is sour milk with sugar.

USA: Dahlys
I live near the Pacific Ocean. I love gardening and watering the vegetables and flowers that grow in our yard. My favourite drinks are water and hot chocolate.

Peru: Lucas
I live high up in the mountains. Our water comes from ice that melts and runs down the mountain. It is really cold here in winter. My favourite drink is home-made lemonade.

# of Water

Bangladesh: Saran
I live in a village surrounded by rivers. In summer it rains so much that sometimes we have floods. I really like to drink fruit juice.

Tajikistan: Barfimoh
I live among hills and mountains. We collect water every day from a spring at the bottom of a hill. I like to drink water, tea and milk.

Contents

Ethiopia: Gamachu
I live in very dry countryside where we need to walk a long way to find water for our cattle. My favourite drink is tea.

Foreword

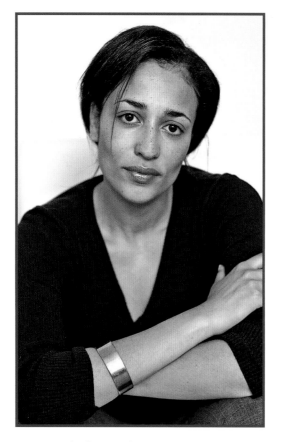

A Book about Water?

This book is about water.

For many people in the developed world, water doesn't seem a very interesting topic. It's everywhere – so obvious and so simple! It flows from our taps into our glasses, into our cooking pots and kettles. It's in our sinks, our baths, our toilets. We don't have to walk very far. We certainly don't have to carry it anywhere. It's in the kitchen, in the bathroom, in a hose in our gardens. Sometimes we even leave it running while we do something else. Some of us have even flushed our toilets to get rid of a single tissue that we couldn't be bothered to put in the bin. When we do things like this we think: *well, it's only water*. Just turn on the tap and there it is!

We forget what a miracle water is. We forget that it supports everything that lives: humans, animals, plants; the sea, the rivers, the mountains; the atmosphere, the air; when we study other planets in the solar system we know for certain that only those with water could ever have sustained life. Without water, we're nothing at all. Unfortunately, sometimes we take this fact for granted. We have a funny human habit of valuing only what seems rare to us, things like masterpieces of art, or diamonds. We think that water is so very common that we needn't value it so highly. But as this book shows, water is not at all as common as we like to think, and we need to value it just as much as paintings and diamonds. Even more, because without it, we cannot live.

The True Value of Water

The children in this book use water in lots of different ways. Apart from drinking it, they use it for cooking, washing their food, washing themselves, their clothes and anything else that needs to be clean; they give it to the animals they look after, because animals need water to live, just as we do. They use water to grow the plants they need to make their food. Children in the developed world also need water for all of these reasons, even if they don't do all these tasks themselves. Maybe it is only when you do these tasks yourself that you understand the true value of water.

In developed countries, it is easy to think of a tap as a magical thing, out of which flows an endless supply of clean water – and all you have do is turn it on. In fact water systems in developed countries rely on many people behind the scenes who recycle, cleanse and reuse our water, and so make sure that we always have what seems like more than enough. But we should still look after it: it takes energy, time and space to cleanse the water. And it is not unlimited. Climate change is causing weather and rainfall patterns to change, which means that many people won't be able to rely on the rain in the way they did before.

A reliable and local supply of fresh water and good sanitation would enhance the lives of millions of people in developing countries. It would protect them from illnesses, and enable them to spend less time and energy collecting water.

If you are reading this book and have your own plentiful water supply, maybe the stories in here will make you think twice about the way you use water. When I finished this book I walked out into the streets of the city I live in – a city that rains plentifully in the wintertime, that is full of fountains, that has a river running straight through it – and I realised that suddenly all the water I could see looked incredibly precious. When I got home I made a list of all the ways I could be less wasteful with the water I use. I think that whenever I am tempted again to think *well, it's only water,* I will pick up this book and take a lesson from the children you are about to meet, because they know better.

Zadie Smith
Rome, Italy.

Peru

Lucas Riquelme lives in Macusani, a small town high up in the mountains of Peru. His family has always farmed alpacas for their wool, but when Lucas grows up, he wants to be a civil engineer. At the moment, Macusani's water comes from melted ice that runs down from the top of the mountains, but climate change is causing the glaciers to shrink so there is less water.

Lucas and his younger brother and sister all love home-made lemonade: water with sugar and fresh lemon juice. Lucas's mother makes it for them at the family's small grocery store in the centre of town. She runs the shop while Lucas's father looks after the animals.

"Whenever I drink water, I always put lemon in it."

Winter in the mountains is freezing cold. His house has no heating or hot water, so first thing in the morning, Lucas washes his face and hands very quickly. When it is time for a bath, his mother heats water on the stove.

Sometimes there are cuts in the water supply and the taps don't work. Lucas and his family collect water and keep it in buckets and bowls in the hallway in case this happens.

"Water is important. It is what gives life!"

Lucas needs a big, hot breakfast to keep him warm at school in the very cold weather. He eats rice, fried cheese, beef, potatoes and salad. To drink, he has a cup of thin porridge.

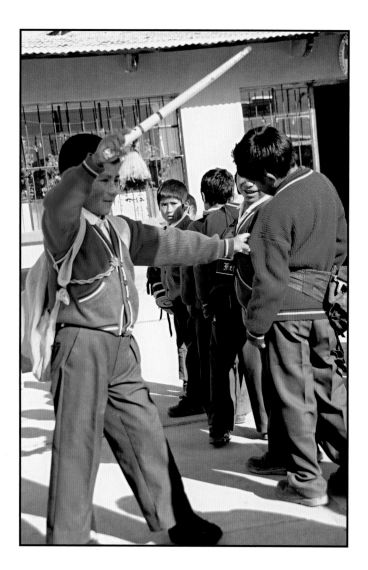

Lucas is proud of his special white baton and the gold braid he wears on his school uniform. They show that he is the class brigadier. He is in charge of getting all his classmates to line up for the morning roll-call.

At school, Lucas learns about how water is used in farming, and how climate change is making a difference to daily life. The mountain above Macusani used to be white, completely covered with snow and ice. Today, he can see most of the bare mountain.

Lucas lives a short walk from his school, so there is always time for a game of football with his friends before and after lessons and during break. He's a big fan of the Brazilian national team.

"We have to wash our hands and faces after playing football. The water is freezing cold!"

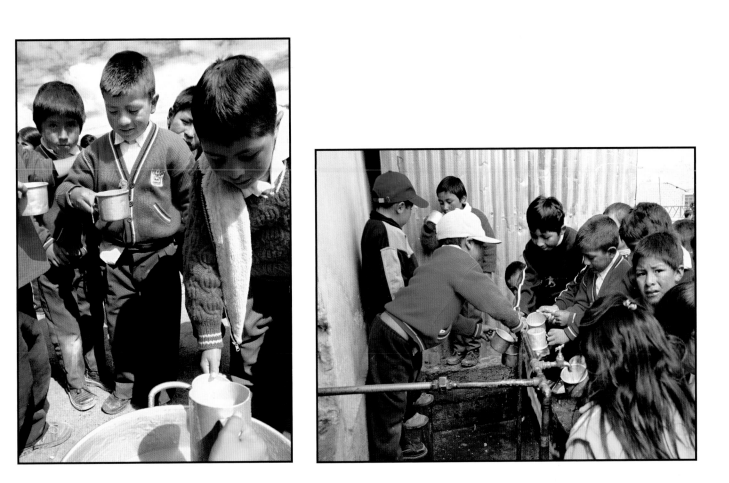

At break time, the children have biscuits and a cup of porridge. Lucas is
hungry after playing football in the cold wind, so he queues up for more
if there is any left over. He has to wash his mug before giving it back.

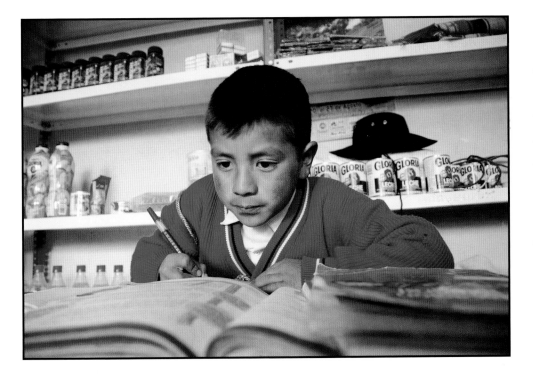

After school, Lucas does
his homework behind
the counter at the
family grocery store.
There's time for another
game of football before
it gets too cold and dark
to play outdoors.

A special time for Lucas – a weekend at the ranch

Lucas looks forward to the weekend, when he goes to the family ranch, higher up the mountain. His father farms a herd of eight hundred alpacas. Lucas keeps warm in the icy weather in his jumper and traditional Peruvian hat made from natural brown and white alpaca wool.

"This is the alpaca capital of the world!"

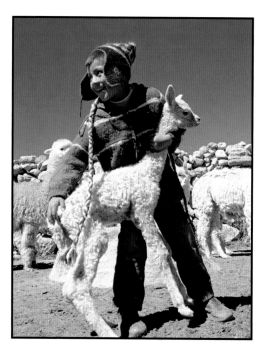

Although he has a special pet alpaca called Oscar, Lucas enjoys looking after all the herd. He helps to give them medicine, check their teeth and make sure their fleece is free of ticks. The alpacas use highland marshes as their watering holes.

"Oscar always comes running when he sees me. He eats leaves out of my hand."

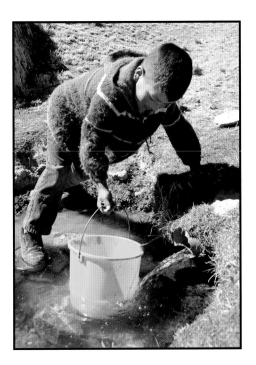

The farmhouse has no running water or cooker. Lucas is in charge of fetching water from a nearby stream. He takes a bucket to collect water every time it's needed, so it is always fresh.

"There's a spring at the top of the hill. My dad put in this pipe to bring the water closer to the house."

Lucas also helps his mother to wash clothes. He lights the fire to heat water and helps to fill the plastic tubs with warm water.

"I help to scrub the clothes, then I lay them on rocks to dry in the wind and sun."

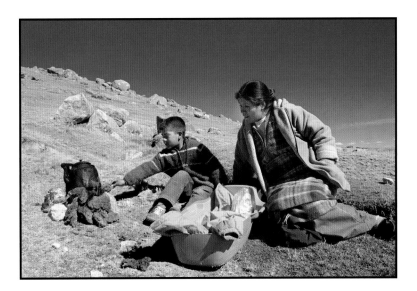

Pedro is the family's alpaca herder. When they have finished their chores, he takes Lucas fishing on a nearby lake. They use poles to push their raft into the water, then they look for a good place to drop their net.

"Water is especially important in the countryside. We need it for the alpacas."

Mauritania

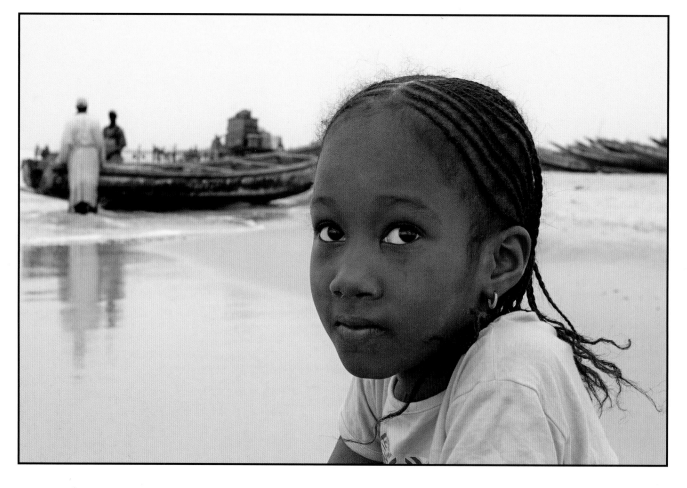

Khadija Sow is eight years old. She lives near the sea
in Mauritania in North Africa. Her home is in Nouakchott,
the capital city. It is hot and sandy because the wind
blows from the Sahara Desert.

Khadija lives with her four-year-old sister,
Aîcha, her mother, grandfather and
grandmother, aunts, uncles and cousins.
Her father is away working in Tunisia.
Khadija and her sister talk to him every
day on the phone.

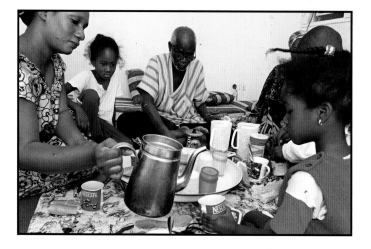

It hardly ever rains, so water is precious. Khadija's family stores drinking water in a big pottery jar. It stands in a shady corner of the courtyard inside their house and keeps their water cool in the hot weather. Khadija takes a drink from the jar when she is thirsty. Some people buy their water in metal barrels, but Khadija's house has running water. There is one tap inside the house. All day long, people use this tap to fill buckets, bowls and kettles, to top up the storage jar, and to wash and cook. Dirty water is carried outside and tipped into a drain close to the house.

"When the weather is hot, I drink a lot of water. Everyone does. We have to keep filling the storage jar."

Brightly-coloured kettles are used for washing hands at mealtimes and to wash before prayer. The kettles are plastic, so they can't go on the gas stove. Water for tea is heated in metal kettles. The tea is made with fresh mint leaves and lots of sugar, and drinking it is an important part of daily life. But Khadija prefers chocolate milk made from powdered milk and water.

"We don't use lots of water. If I spoil water by making it dirty, my mother will be very cross with me. Other people need it for washing and drinking, so we mustn't waste water."

School is just a few minutes' walk away, and Khadija enjoys maths and French. When they are thirsty at school, the children dip a cup into a bucket. That way, they don't waste the water from the tap.

"If the water in the bucket looks spoilt, then I go to the tap instead."

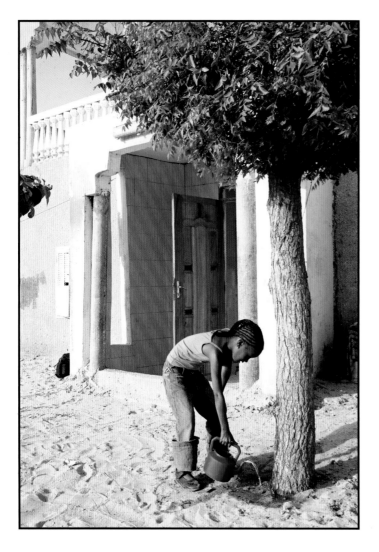

Khadija comes home for lunch. She eats some fish and rice. In the evening she waters the two trees outside the house. Her older cousin, Mbolou, feeds and waters the family's animals.

"The sheep drink a lot of water. We give them the water we have used for washing rice. We catch the water that drips from the storage jar and use it to water the trees. We need the trees for shade from the sun."

Khadija's favourite place is the beach outside the town. Her family sometimes goes there for a picnic. Khadija knows how to swim, but she is nervous of the waves, so she just paddles today. At the fisherman's beach nearby, Khadija's aunt buys fish that has just been landed from the wooden fishing boats.

"We swim, and then we eat, and then we swim, and then we eat again. The sea is water, but we can't drink it."

A special time for Khadija – celebrating Tabaski

Eid al-Adha or 'the Festival of Sacrifice' is an important part of the Islamic calendar. In Mauritania, the three-day festival is called *Tabaski*. It is traditional to kill a ram and the meat is later cooked and eaten. Khadija and her sister watch the ram being washed as part of the ceremony. Like other families who can afford it, Khadija's family celebrates by sharing their food with poorer families.

Khadija helps to wash all the family's clothes before Tabaski. For the festival, everyone wears new clothes that they have bought or received as gifts. Khadija changes her clothes as often as her mother will let her.

As part of the dressing up for the festival, Khadija has her hands and feet decorated with patterns painted in henna, a vegetable dye. She has her hair washed and goes to the hairdresser to have it specially styled.

"I don't like having my hair washed. The soap gets in my eyes, and the comb pulls my hair until it hurts."

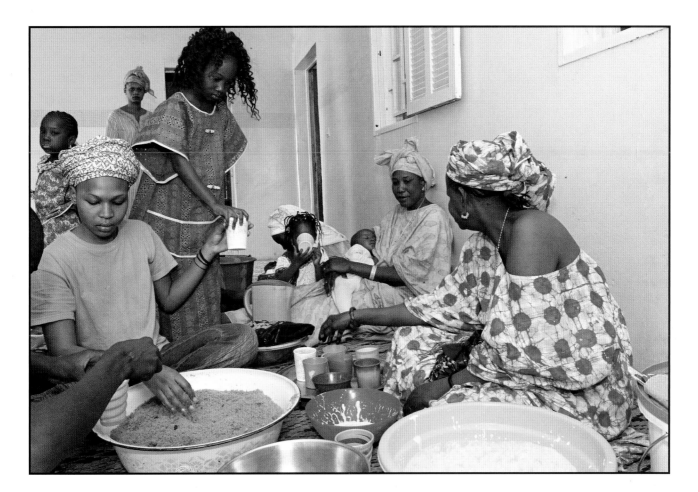

Khadija enjoys a special holiday meal called *thieboudjen*. A whole fish is served with spicy rice and vegetables – carrots, radish, yellow peppers and cabbage. Afterwards, she has a drink made of boiled rice and milk called *gossi*.

"My favourite drink is tufam. It is sour milk and sugar. We drink it when the weather is hot, because it makes you feel fresh when you are tired."

Khadija and her friends go from house to house asking friends and relatives for gifts. Visitors who come to their house also give them small gifts and money.

"I will spend all my money on cake and fizzy drinks. At the market they pour our drinks into plastic bags."

USA

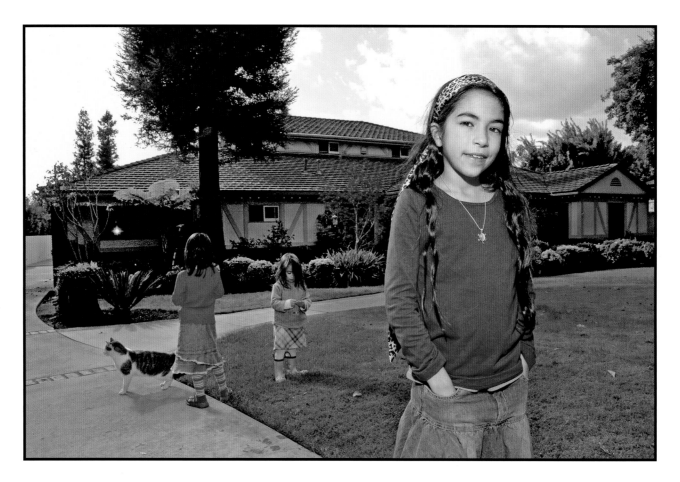

Dahlys Ang lives in a town called Arcadia, near Los Angeles City in California. Her home is not far from the Pacific Ocean, but the climate is very dry, because of the mountains to the north and the Mojave Desert to the east. It hardly ever rains, so extra water has to be pumped in from the Colorado River.

Dahlys lives with her parents and two younger sisters. Her father works as an accountant and her mother stays at home. Her family eats dinner together every night – the children take it in turns to say grace. There is always a big jug of water on the table. Each girl drinks from her own beaker – Dahlys has a yellow one.

Even though she only needs to turn on a tap to get as much hot and cold running water as she wants, Dahlys has learned at school that water is precious, especially in places where there is little rain. She takes care not to leave the tap running when she washes her hands and brushes her teeth.

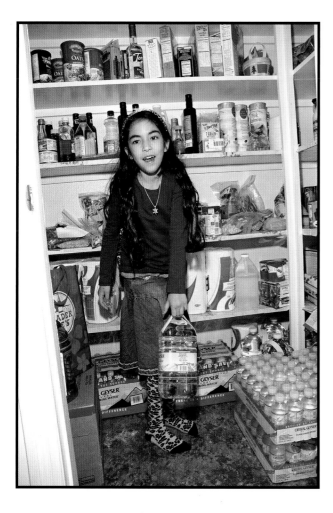

"I only use water to clean my toothbrush, or to rinse the soap off my hands. I remind my parents and sisters to turn off the tap, too."

Dahlys's family also buys water in bottles. She takes a small bottle to school, or when she plays sport. Big bottles are used for drinking and cooking. They also store bottled water in case of an emergency, such as an earthquake, when the water supply might be cut off.

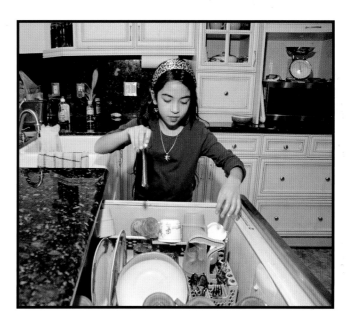

At eight years old, Dahlys is able to help around the house. She loads dirty clothes into the washing machine and stacks the dishwasher with dirty dishes.

Dahlys is in charge of the family pets – two cats and two goldfish. Every day, she feeds the cats and gives them fresh water to drink. She is teaching her sisters how to feed the fish and change the water in their tanks.

"I like watering the plants and feeding the fish. I don't like doing the laundry or rinsing the dishes."

When she is on holiday from school, Dahlys likes to spend time gardening at home. Her mother has made a small vegetable patch in their garden, so Dahlys and her sisters are learning how to grow food. So far, they have grown squashes, cucumbers and tomatoes.

Dahlys saves the water that her mother uses for cooking, so that she can use it later to water the plants. After watering the flowers in the garden, she brings out all the pot plants from the house on to the patio and gives them a good drink of water, too.

"At school I learned that if we don't save water, we will have less for everyone to drink. Now, I remind Mom to save the cooking water for the plants."

When she goes shopping for groceries with her mother, Dahlys likes to stop to look at the flowers outside the grocery store. They smell so good that she would like to take them all home with her.

Dahlys's mother teaches her how important it is to have clean water. She shows the girls a sign painted on the pavement, on top of the cover for a drain. The sign warns people not to dump anything into the drain, because it carries water into the Pacific Ocean.

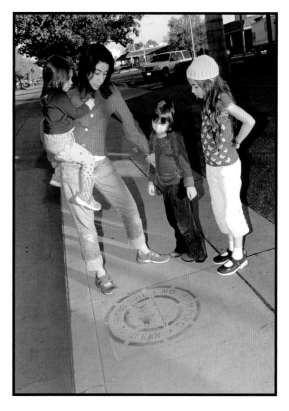

The beach is not far from where Dahlys lives, and she loves going there in the summer.

"Every day at sunset we go swimming in the sea, then we play on the sand and collect shells. I like floating in the ocean."

A special day for Dahlys – a hike with Dad

Dahlys and her sisters enjoy helping to wash the family car at the weekend. They use just one bucket of soapy water before they rinse the car with the hose-pipe and polish it dry. Then Dahlys and her father drive off in their clean and shiny car to go for a hike in the mountains.

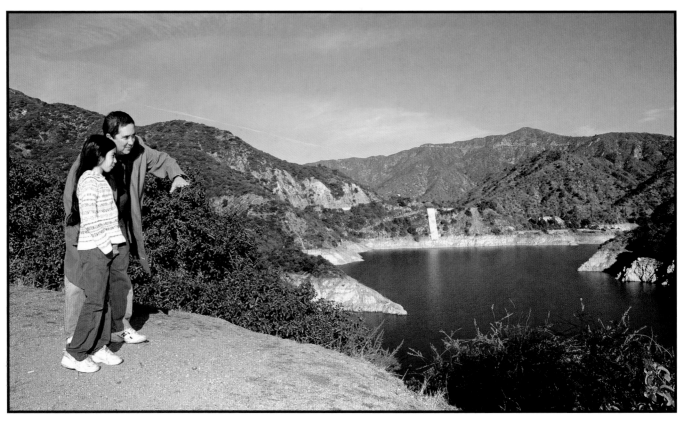

The mountain land is extremely dry and very little grows there. Because this part of southern California is so dry, water is pumped in from northern California and from the Colorado River. There are two big water reservoirs up here in the mountains, but they don't store much water because there isn't enough rain to fill them up. Dahlys's father tells her that the water level used to be much higher than it is today.

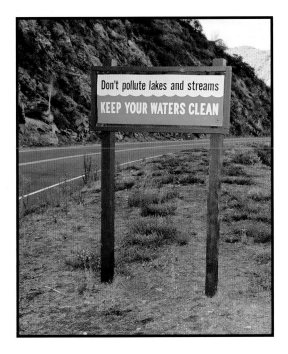

The mountain scenery is beautiful, and Dahlys and her dad have fun walking together. But she is sad to see that some people dump junk here. Dahlys's father explains that rubbish left around the lakes will pollute the water. Dahlys reads a sign that tells visitors that the water they see here may come out of their taps tomorrow, so they should take care to keep the water clean.

"My wish about water is that people would stop throwing rubbish in the ocean, and keep the water clean for everyone. If you see rubbish near the lake, or on the beach, you should pick it up and take it away so that it doesn't go in the water."

Dahlys is hot and tired after her long hike in the mountains. When she gets home, she is very happy to jump into the swimming pool and enjoy the cool, refreshing water with her father and sisters.

Bangladesh

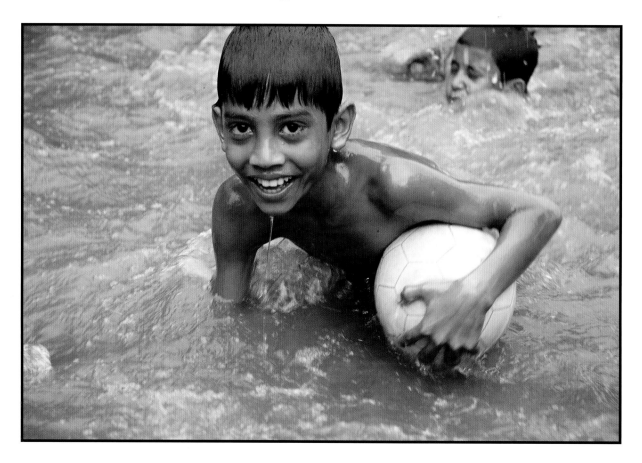

Mohammed Golam Sadik Saran (or Saran for short) lives in Gaibandha in northern Bangladesh. The village where he lives is surrounded by rivers, so the land is very fertile. Most people are farmers or fishermen. It is hot and rainy in summer, and sometimes the rivers flood. Saran loves to splash in the ponds near his home, or take a boat on the river.

Saran is eight years old. He lives with his parents and two older brothers, as well as some of his aunts, uncles, grandparents and younger cousins. His father owns a pharmacy in the town and he also shares a farm with Saran's uncles. They grow sugar cane, potatoes, onions, eggplant, okra, garlic and ginger. Saran's house has a big courtyard where grain is laid out to dry after it is harvested.

"We have a machine that goes deep into the ground and pumps water for all the farmland. I help to scatter the seeds for the crops. Sometimes I water the plants and plant the seeds into the ground."

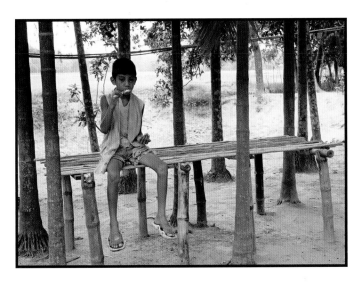

Because it is so hot, Saran likes to wash three times a day, before school, when he gets home in the afternoon and before he goes to bed. He also washes his own shirt after school. He brushes his teeth three times a day.

"I use four big mugs of water for my morning wash, and one mug in the afternoon and evening."

Saran collects water for his wash from one of the three pumps in his home. These are called tube wells and they pump up water from underground. The water is used for bathing, washing clothes, cooking and drinking. Clothes are washed outdoors, first in the ponds that belong to Saran's family, then a second time in fresh water from the tube wells.

"When you pump the handle of the tube well, water comes out. You collect it in a bucket, mug or water bottle."

After eating some rice for breakfast, Saran gets a ride to school on a rickshaw. The school is in the main town, too far for Saran to walk there from his home.

Saran brings drinking water from home in a plastic bottle. When the bottle is empty, he fills it up from one of the taps and tube wells at school.

Saran keeps cool by splashing his face with water from a tube well in the playground. The playground is sprayed with water to stop the wind blowing dust and sand into the classrooms.

"It is so hot! I drink lots of water, because I feel so thirsty."

When he gets home, Saran has a snack of rice with sugar and milk and a short nap before doing his homework. He also helps on the farm, giving the calves a drink and looking after the pigeons.

"We have cattle, sheep, hens, ducks and pigeons. They all need lots of water."

The pigeons are Saran's favourites. Sometimes an injured bird falls into the pond, and Saran must jump in to rescue it before it drowns.

Saran finds thunder and lightning scary, especially at night, but he enjoys the rain. He likes to walk around the farm, looking at the animals and birds.

"When there is too much rain, the river bursts its banks and there are floods. There is water everywhere. Houses can be flooded and people can drown."

A special day for Saran – a family trip to the river

Today is Friday, a day of rest. Saran is excited because the whole family is going on a trip to the river. He likes to keep his room clean and tidy, so he makes his bed and sweeps it with a broom made of reeds.

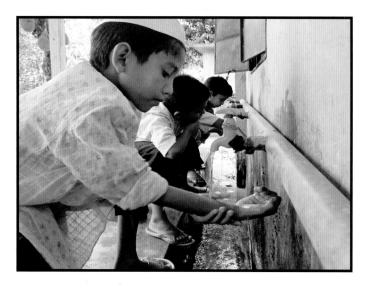

Saran walks with his father and brothers to the nearby mosque. Following the Muslim custom, he washes his face, hands and feet before prayer.

Later, he enjoys a special meal of chicken with spices, fish, rice, vegetables and sweet cakes.

After a short nap, Saran is ready to have fun. He is good at drawing and singing, but his favourite game is cricket. Sometimes he and his friends play for hours. They get hot and dusty after a long game, then they run and jump straight into the nearby pond.

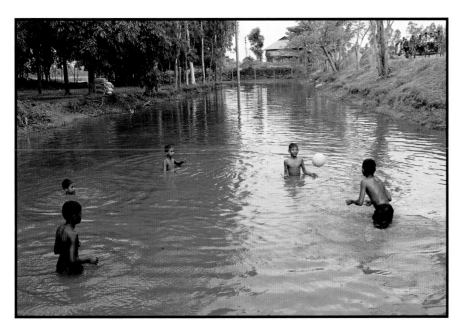

"My friends and I splash each other and we play with a ball. Sometimes I go into the ponds and collect water hyacinths with my own hands."

In the evening, everyone dresses up for a sunset boat trip on the river. They visit small islands which sink below the water when the river is full and appear again in the dry season. Saran is happy to be on the water with his family, watching the fishermen casting their nets.

"Water is another name for life. We drink water, we go in boats and we catch fish. My favourite thing about water is swimming."

Ethiopia

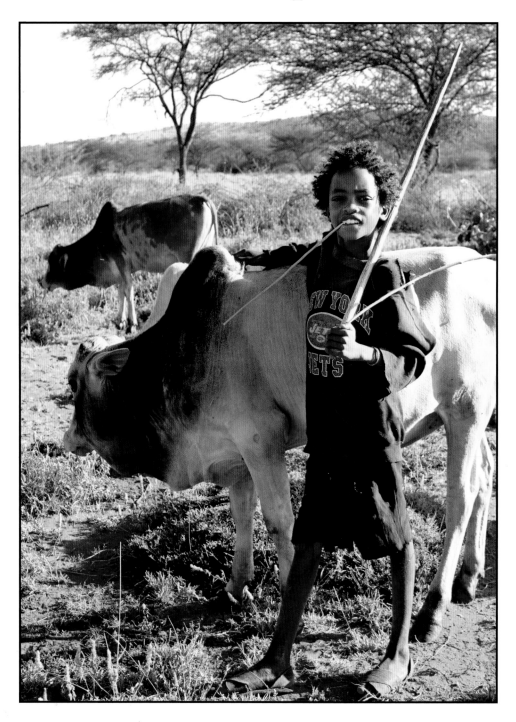

Although Gamachu Boru is only seven years old, he has an important job looking after animals. He lives in a village in southern Ethiopia, where it is very dry. Gamachu belongs to the Borana people who keep cattle, camels, goats, sheep and, sometimes, horses. Water and grazing for the animals are the most important parts of their lives.

Gamachu lives with his parents, three sisters, and brother, as well as his sister's two children. The calves sleep inside with the family until they are about two years old, to keep them safe from wild animals. All the children help by taking the family's animals out to find water.

"I don't go to school because I look after the calves. When my brother is old enough to look after them by himself, then I will go to school."

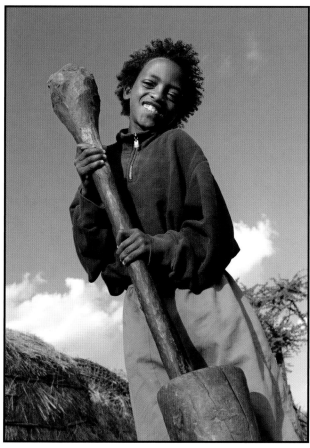

It is difficult to grow food because there is so little rain, so Gamachu's family usually buys their maize (a type of corn). Gamachu eats maize porridge when he gets back from his day with the calves.

"I grind the maize every day, then my mother separates the kernel from the husks. She puts a pot of water on the fire and adds the maize to it."

Everyone in the Borana community spends most of their time walking to and from the water-holes. In the dry season, the men are sometimes away for days with the animals. The women and girls collect water for the family's washing and cooking. Gamachu's mother walks for three hours twice a day to fetch water from the nearest pond. Donkeys help to carry the heavy water containers.

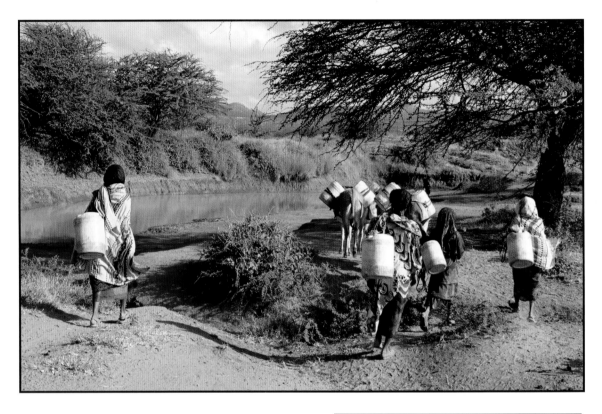

Early every morning, Gamachu sets off with the calves for the pond. He is out for more than ten hours and doesn't come back until the sun sets. He takes a bottle with a little milk for his lunch. He will add water to the milk when he reaches the pond, to make it last longer and to quench his thirst better.

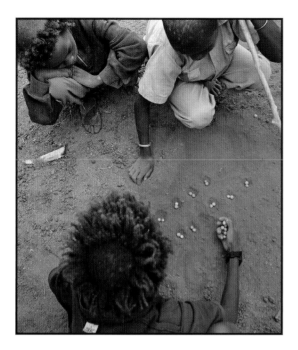

Gamachu meets up with friends who are also looking after their families' animals. They play games while the calves graze.

"I like playing toki (jacks). We wrestle, we sing, we swim in the pond and we make animals from clay. We make camels, cattle and horses."

A stick from an andarak or an adea plant makes a good toothbrush. Gamachu knows how to find the right plants. He doesn't need water to clean his teeth this way.

"I take a stick with me when I go with the calves, or I find one on the way to the pond."

When he gets to the pond, he has a wash and fills up his bottle with water. The ponds are only there when there is enough rainwater to fill them. When the ponds dry up, everyone has to walk much further to get water from the deep wells.

"During the rainy season the ponds fill up, there is plenty of milk to drink, the cattle don't have to go so far to get water and I don't get tired."

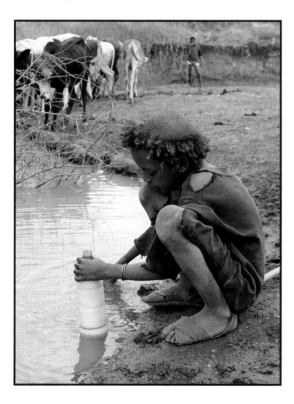

A special day for Gamachu – a walk to the 'singing wells'

The pond nearest to Gamachu's home has now dried up, so he must go with his father to take the cattle to the deep wells further away. Gamachu shares early morning tea with his family before he sets out with his father on the long walk.

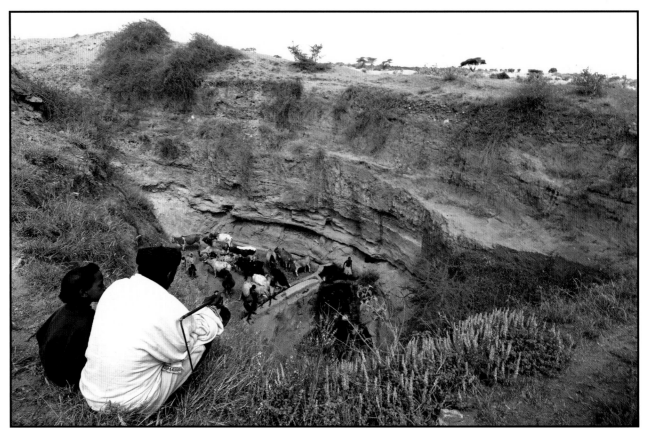

The wells are busy in the dry season. When they arrive, Gamachu and his father sit at the top and watch for a while. The animals have to drink in a certain order: horses first, donkeys, then cattle, and camels last of all.

"When there is no water, I wish for water."

A group of people makes a human chain to pass the water in buckets from deep down in the well up the steep walls to the top. Those at the top pour it into drinking troughs for the animals. The name 'singing wells' comes from the songs they chant as they pass the pails from person to person. This helps them work fast and keep a rhythm as they swing the full buckets up the well and lower the empty ones back down to the bottom to be filled again. The human chain works faster than a machine.

When their cattle have finished drinking, Gamachu guides them away from the well.

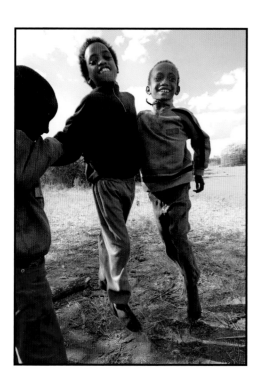

"Water is good for everything. The crops grow, it's good for drinking, the grass grows fast and the cattle don't have to go too far, so they become fat very quickly."

Even after his long walk home from the 'singing wells', Gamachu still has enough energy to play and dance with his friends.

Tajikistan

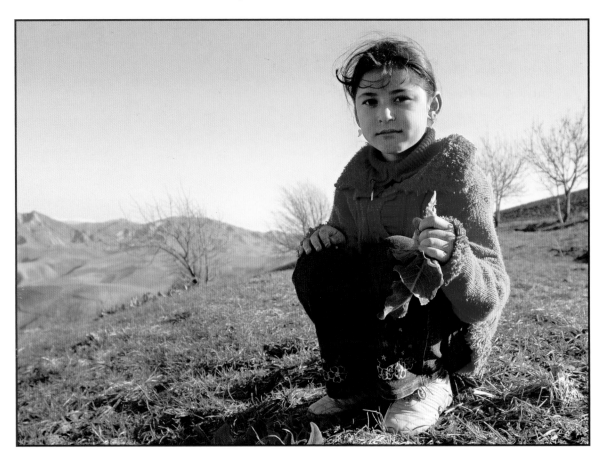

Barfimoh Rajabova's first name means snow and moon, because she was born in snowy weather. She lives in Tajikistan, the smallest country in Central Asia, which has some of the highest mountains in the world. Barfimoh's village is near the border with Afghanistan.

At eight years old, Barfimoh is the youngest in her family. She lives with her mother and father, some of her ten brothers and sisters and their children – Barfimoh's nieces and nephews. Like most people in Tajikistan, her family are farmers.

Early in the morning, Barfimoh has a wash and brushes her teeth with warm water. There is no running water in the village so Barfimoh and her sisters must collect their water from a spring at the bottom of a steep hill. She loves eggs from the family's chickens and eats as many as she can. She even brings some to eat on the journey.

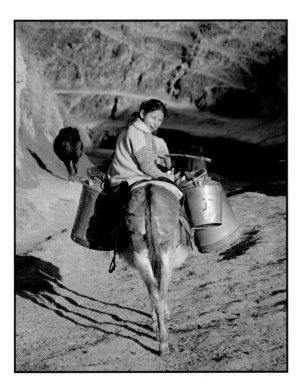

"Chickens need water, or they can't make eggs."

When the weather is warmer, the family stores all the water they collect in a concrete well. In the cold winter, the water would freeze in the well, so they keep it in pots in the woodshed instead.

"We take our donkey and two big containers. There is a tap and a bucket at the spring. I fill the bucket, then my sister pours it into the containers. It takes about eight buckets to fill them both."

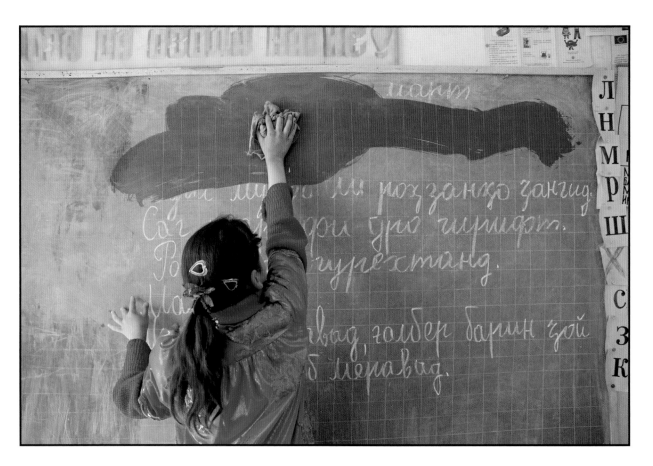

At school, Barfimoh likes to clean the blackboard. The water is kept in a large tin container that hangs on a pole outside the building. The school cleaners bring the water from their homes every day.

"My teacher says we must save water, boil water for drinking, and wash our hands after using the toilet."

When she gets home from school, Barfimoh plays with her favourite lamb. Barfimoh likes to help with the farm animals which live outdoors behind her house, but she isn't strong enough yet to carry the heavy buckets of water for them to drink.

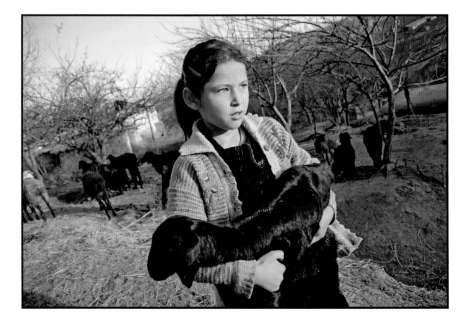

At home, Barfimoh's sisters do the cooking, the washing up and the laundry. They try to use as little water as possible. They heat the water in a wood-fired clay oven.

Barfimoh helps her father in the kitchen garden. The family collects rainwater that runs off the roof of their home. They use it to water their wheat, potatoes, onions, tomatoes, peas and melon.

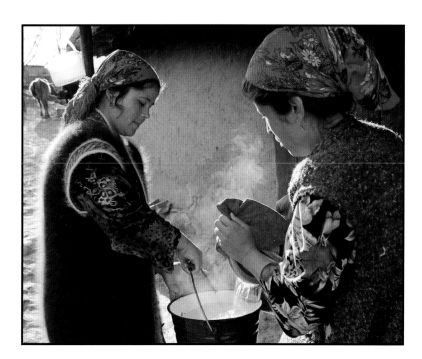

"He digs and then I plant the potatoes in their beds. If the potatoes don't get water, they won't grow — they'll stay under the ground."

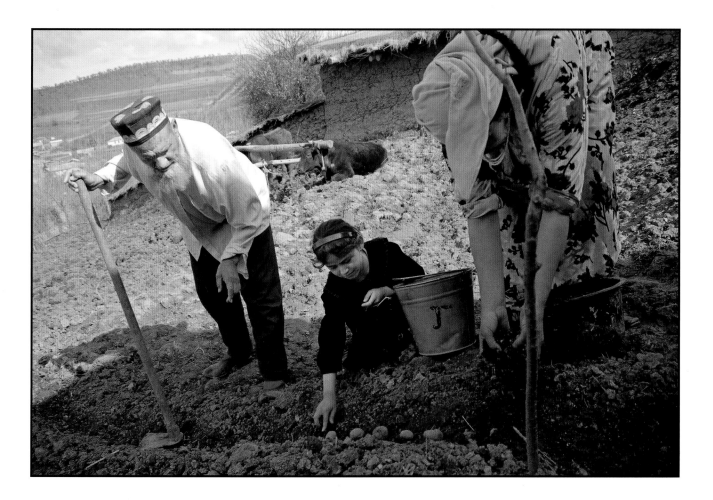

A special time for Barfimoh – the Spring festival of Navruz

Every year on the first day of spring, Barfimoh's village celebrates the ancient festival of Navruz. It means 'new day' and marks the return of life after the cold of winter. Everyone dresses in their brightest clothes for a day of music, dancing and feasting.

"My favourite seasons are spring and summer."

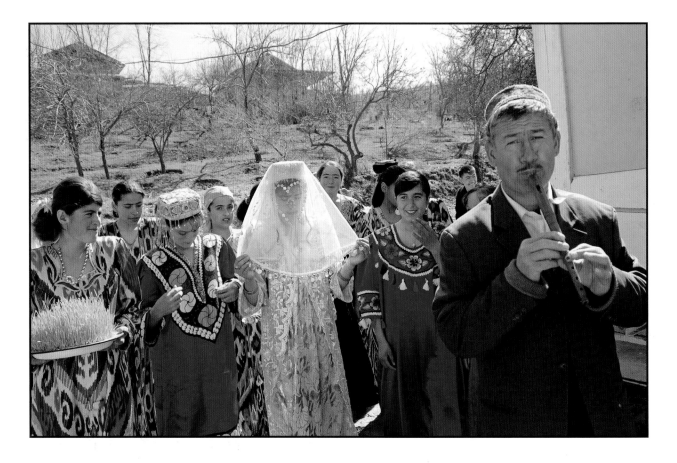

Navruz is called 'the season of the bride'. A schoolgirl dresses up as a bride to represent spring. Her attendants carry a platter of sprouted wheat. Sprouted grains are one of the special Navruz foods. They are seen as a symbol of life and health.

Each class in Barfimoh's school prepares a Navruz dish. The children lay out the feast on carpets on the school playing field and the whole village joins in.

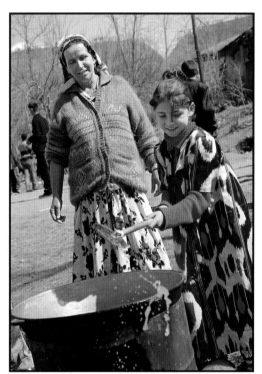

Barfimoh enjoys dancing with her friends before she eats freshly baked bread and *dalda*, a soup of fresh herbs, beans and peas. After the feast, Barfimoh helps to clean out the big cooking pots.

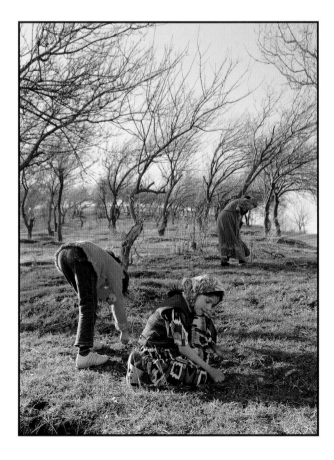

The two-week holiday is a time to plough the fields and sow seeds, spring-clean homes and cook special dishes using the new crops of spring. Barfimoh's favourite part of the holiday is going into the mountains for the first time in the year to pick herbs.

"Where I live it is very beautiful. If there was no rain, the trees would not be green, the wheat would not grow, the hills would be yellow."

43

What do you know about water?

Water can contain germs, so many people have to boil it or find other ways to purify it before they can drink it. Tea, coffee, soup, beer and wine were originally ways to quench thirst without the risks of drinking dirty water.

A tap that drips once a second can waste 4 litres of water a day.

Springs and other natural sources of fresh water have to be protected to make sure that the water stays clean.

Water covers 75% of our planet's surface and 75% of the human body is also made up water.

In richer countries, water is stored in reservoirs before being supplied to people's homes. The first major water storage reservoir in the world was built in 450 BC in South America and was still in use in the 19th century.

The oceans hold 97% of the world's water. 2% is frozen in the polar ice caps. That means only 1% of the world's water is available for all our needs.

2.6 billion people in the world have no access to clean latrines or toilets. 1.8 million children die every year as a result of diseases caused by unclean water and poor sanitation. That's 5,000 deaths a day.

1.1 billion people in the world don't have access to clean water. That's about one in every six people.

In poorer countries, women and girls can spend up to six hours each day collecting enough water for their families to use. The heavy containers can give them back pain and other health problems.

A person can live for several weeks without food, but only days without water.

Glossary

Peru

Alpaca – a South American mammal with long, soft hair.

Civil engineer – a job concerned with designing, building or repairing roads, bridges or tunnels.

Class brigadier – like a class captain; a child given responsibilities for keeping his or her classmates in order.

Climate change – a term used to describe long-term changes in the weather or seasons, meaning that some places are wetter or drier than they used to be, and some parts of the world are hotter or colder.

Glacier – a very slowly moving frozen river or mass of ice.

Tick – an insect that sucks blood from the skin of warm-blooded animals. They must be removed as they can pass on diseases.

Mauritania

Eid al-Adha – a festival when Muslims remember the story of Ibrahim's (Abraham's) sacrifice.

Gossi – a drink made of boiled rice and milk.

Henna – a red plant dye that is used to colour hair and decorate skin.

Ram – a male sheep.

Sahara Desert – a vast desert that covers a large part of North Africa, from the Atlantic Ocean to the River Nile in Egypt.

Storage jar – a large pottery jar that is used to keep fresh water cool and clean.

Tabaski – the name for Eid al-Adha in some West African countries.

Thieboudjen – a fish dish with spicy rice and vegetables, served as part of the Tabaski celebrations.

Tufam – a drink made with sour milk and sugar.

USA

Colorado River – a river that flows through the south-west of the USA into Mexico. It is over 2,000 kilometres long.

Dishwasher – a machine for washing dishes.

Drains – an underground system of tunnels that carries water away to rivers or seas.

Earthquake – a shaking of the ground, caused by volcanic activity or pressure from deep beneath the Earth's surface. Earthquakes often damage buildings, and electricity and water supplies.

Grace – a Christian prayer of thanks for food, spoken before a meal.

Hose-pipe – a tube attached to a tap and used to carry water.

Mojave Desert – A desert in southern California and parts of Nevada, Utah and Arizona. It covers almost 60,000 square kilometres.

Pacific Ocean – the largest of the Earth's oceans, stretching from Asia and Australia to North and South America.

Pollute – to make air, land or water dirty or unhealthy.

Reservoir – an artificial lake used to collect and store water to supply a town or city.

Squash – a vegetable with fibres and seeds. Pumpkin is a type of squash.

Swimming pool – a tank, usually made of concrete, filled with water and used for swimming.

Washing machine – a machine for washing clothes.

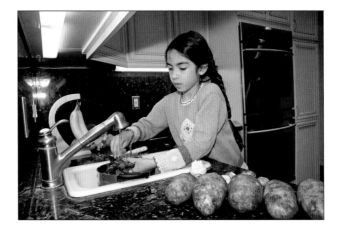

Bangladesh

Crops – plants which produce food, such as rice or wheat, or other useful produce, such as cotton.

Eggplant – a dark purple fruit that is eaten as a vegetable; also known as aubergine.

Fertile – land or soil where plants grow easily.

Flood – when rivers, seas or lakes burst their banks, causing water to flow into buildings and across roads. If the dirty water gets into fresh water supplies, it can cause disease.

Garlic – a plant, part of the onion family. The root has a strong smell and is used to add flavour in cooking.

Ginger – a plant with a spicy root used for cooking and medicine.

Harvest – the gathering of crops when they are ready.

Mosque – the Muslim place of worship.

Muslim – a follower of Islam.

Okra – a thin, green vegetable, sometimes called *ladies' fingers*.

Rickshaw – a kind of tricycle which carries one or two passengers.

Sugar cane – the plant from which refined sugar is made.

Sweet cakes – cakes made with sugar, eaten as snacks or dessert.

Tube well – a pump that brings water from wells deep underground.

Water hyacinth – like a water lily, a plant with flowers that float on the water.

Ethiopia

Graze – how cattle, horses, sheep or other plant-eating animals feed.

Kernel – the centre of a nut or the stone of a fruit.

Maize – a type of corn.

Singing wells – deep wells where people chant songs as they pass water up the steep sides in buckets.

Toki – a game like jacks.

Trough – a long, narrow container used for feeding or watering animals.

Water-hole – a natural pond or pool used by people and animals.

Tajikistan

Spring – a source of fresh water that naturally flows from underground.

Melon – a large fruit that grows on a vine. It has a thick rind and sweet, juicy flesh.

Navruz – a festival that celebrates the arrival of spring.

Platter – a large, shallow plate used for serving food.

Dalda – a soup made of herbs.

Index